MONUMENTAL MILESTONES
GREAT EVENTS OF MODERN TIMES

Brown v. Board of Education of Topeka, Kansas, 1954

White Americans march against the integration of Central High School in Little Rock, Arkansas, on the steps of the Supreme Court building in Washington, D.C.

Mitchell Lane
PUBLISHERS
P.O. Box 196
Hockessin, Delaware 19707

Titles in the Series

MONUMENTAL MILESTONES
GREAT EVENTS OF MODERN TIMES

Brown v. Board of Education of Topeka, Kansas, 1954

After the Brown ruling, Ruby Bridges became the first African American student to attend an all-white school in New Orleans.

KaaVonia Hinton

Mitchell Lane

PUBLISHERS

Copyright © 2010 by Mitchell Lane Publishers, Inc. All rights reserved. No part of this book may be reproduced without written permission from the publisher. Printed and bound in the United States of America.

Printing   1   2   3   4   5   6   7   8   9

Library of Congress Cataloging-in-Publication Data
Hinton, KaaVonia, 1973–
  Brown v. Board of Education, Topeka, KS, 1954 / by KaaVonia Hinton.
      p. cm. — (Monumental milestones)
  Includes bibliographical references and index.
  ISBN 978-1-58415-738-0 (library bound)
  1. Brown, Oliver, 1918–1961—Trials, litigation, etc.—Juvenile literature. 2. Topeka (Kan.). Board of Education—Trials, litigation, etc.—Juvenile literature. 3. Segregation in education—Law and legislation—United States—Juvenile literature. [1. African Americans—Civil rights—Juvenile literature.] I. Title.
  KF228.B76H56 2009
  344.73'0798—dc22

                                                                           2009027329

ABOUT THE AUTHOR: KaaVonia Hinton is an assistant professor in the Teaching & Learning department at Old Dominion University in Norfolk, Virginia. She is the author of *Angela Johnson: Poetic Prose* (Scarecrow Press), *Sharon M. Draper: Embracing Literacy* (Scarecrow Press) and, for Mitchell Lane Publishers, *Jacqueline Woodson* and *The Underground Railroad.*

PUBLISHER'S NOTE: This story is based on the author's extensive research, which she believes to be accurate. Documentation of such research is contained on page 45.
    The internet sites referenced herein were active as of the publication date. Due to the fleeting nature of some web sites, we cannot guarantee they will all be active when you are reading this book.

Contents

Brown v. Board of Education of Topeka, Kansas, 1954

*For Your Information

Linda Brown (right) sitting in a classroom with other African American students in Monroe Elementary School in 1953. Like so many others, the school was overcrowded, understaffed, and underfunded.

In 1951, African Americans sued the Board of Education of Topeka, Kansas, when it tried to segregate the junior high schools. They won the lawsuit, but the elementary schools remained segregated. Linda never got the opportunity to attend an integrated elementary school.

Briggs v. Clarendon County, South Carolina

People all over the world admire the U.S. school system. After the Civil War, the country began offering all children an opportunity to go to school to learn how to read, write, and become responsible citizens. During the 1900s, some children found it hard to take advantage of this opportunity. African American children, especially those living in the South, were rarely able to attend school during the farming season, and many eventually stopped attending school after third or fourth grade because they had to help support their families.

During the early years of the American educational system, schools were segregated; there were black schools and white schools. African American children who were able to attend elementary, junior high, or high school attended schools that were for African American students. When these students wanted to attend schools for white children, they were not allowed. Sometimes parents—like Sarah Roberts's father, Benjamin F. Roberts—sued. Roberts lost the case, *Roberts v. the City of Boston*, but it is an important case for many reasons.

In 1896, *Roberts v. the City of Boston* was used to support the ruling of *Plessy v. Ferguson*, which said segregation was legal. Even though the laws in the United States said schools must be separate but equal, white schools had better books and materials, plenty of teachers, new buildings, and school buses. African American schools often had used books and materials, few teachers, crowded classrooms, leaky roofs, and no buses.

The National Association for the Advancement of Colored People (NAACP) believed segregated schools were unfair. The NAACP decided to use the law to fight for better conditions in African American schools. In the

early 1900s, the organization began hiring lawyers. One of the lawyers, Charles Hamilton Houston, believed the NAACP would be more successful if lawyers challenged segregation at the university level before attacking it in elementary and high schools. To help him fight against separate and unequal schools, he chose attorneys from among those he had trained at Howard University. One of them was Thurgood Marshall.

After Houston, Thurgood Marshall, and other lawyers who worked for the NAACP began fighting against segregation in universities and winning, they started to look for African American families who had children in public schools that were not equal to white schools. They wanted the families to file lawsuits that challenged segregation. The NAACP wanted cases from different parts of the United States so that they could prove that African American students attended unequal schools in many parts of the country, not just in the South. These cases were called test cases. The NAACP lawyers planned to eventually argue that separate schools could never be equal and that segregation

Supreme Court Justice
Thurgood Marshall

Marshall was the chief lawyer of the NAACP's Legal Defense and Education Fund for many years. In 1967 he became the first African American appointed to serve as a Supreme Court Justice.

violated the Fourteenth Amendment, which says all citizens should receive "equal protection under the laws."[1]

Brown v. Board of Education of Topeka, Kansas, is one of the well-known Supreme Court Cases the NAACP used to fight for better schools for African Americans. *Brown* included five cases from four states (South Carolina, Kansas, Delaware, and Virginia) and the District of Columbia. These cases were grouped together by the Supreme Court. The five cases were called *Brown* because the *Brown* case was listed first, but the *Brown* case was not the first one in the group that the NAACP worked on. The first case in the group was *Briggs v. Elliott*. It was argued in Charleston, South Carolina, in May 1951.

Joseph Albert DeLaine, an African American minister and teacher in Clarendon County, South Carolina, encouraged twenty parents to sue for desegregation. The names on the lawsuit were listed in alphabetical order. Since Harry Briggs's name was listed first, the case is named after him. *Elliott* is Roderick W. Elliott, the chairman of School District No. 22, where the parents' children went to school. Schools were separate and unequal in Clarendon County. The African American teachers earned less money than the white teachers who did the same job, and white schools received nearly three times more money per student than African American schools received. The officials in Clarendon County argued that since white people paid more taxes than African American people did, they had the right to spend "$179 per white child in the public schools [while] for each black child, they spent $43."[2]

While DeLaine studied at Allen University, he listened to a speaker from the NAACP named James M. Hinton. Hinton said the African American schools in South Carolina were in poor condition and difficult for students to get to because buses were not available for them. He also said the NAACP was already fighting for better schools in Virginia and wanted to extend the fight to South Carolina. The NAACP believed the fight should start with buses. African American citizens should ask school boards to give African American schools buses for its children who were walking as far as nine miles to attend.

Hinton told DeLaine and the other people in the audience, "No teacher or preacher in South Carolina has the courage" to fight for buses for African American schools.[3] Hinton was wrong: There were brave people in South Carolina. DeLaine and two other people went to the school superintendent and asked for buses for African American schools, but they were told African

Americans did not pay enough taxes, "and it was not fair to expect white citizens to [carry] a . . . heavier economic burden by providing transportation" for African Americans.[4] Though the African American community eventually bought a bus, school officials would not provide fuel for it, as the school system did for the buses that took white students to school.

Determined to fight for equal transportation for African American students, DeLaine asked Levi Pearson to take legal action. Though Pearson knew the possible danger involved, he said yes. Pearson lived in Jordan, an area that often flooded. When the roads flooded, "black children had to row a boat" to get to school.[5] When roads were clear, Pearson's children had to walk several miles to get to school. On July 28, 1947, Pearson's lawyer wrote a petition, or a request, for buses and sent it to local school board officials and to the secretary of the State Board of Education. When school officials did not respond, Pearson tried to sue, but his case was thrown out of court because he did not pay taxes to the school district where his children attended school. Though Pearson and his family suffered because whites refused to do business with him, DeLaine and Pearson kept trying to get transportation for African American students.

DeLaine, Pearson, and others met with Thurgood Marshall in Columbia, South Carolina, to discuss what they would do next. The plan was simple. They would get at least twenty people to sue for better schools, not just for buses. Since the *Plessy v. Ferguson* ruling of 1896, schools and other public facilities, such as bathrooms and water fountains, had to be separate but equal. According to historian Richard Kluger, "African Americans were going to ask for equal treatment from top to bottom: buses, buildings, teachers' salaries, teaching materials. Everything the same."[6] Finding enough people willing to put their lives in danger was not so simple, but eight months later DeLaine had the names of twenty African Americans who had grown tired of unfair schools and decided they had to act.

DeLaine, Briggs, and the other people who signed the lawsuit put their lives and their jobs at risk. DeLaine lost his teaching job, and other members of his family lost their jobs, too. DeLaine's house was burned down, and he received death threats. While Briggs said no one threatened to hurt him, his boss at the gas station told him he would fire him if he did not take his name off the lawsuit. Briggs refused because he believed the lawsuit would help children get a better education. Liza Briggs, Harry Briggs' wife, worked at the Summerton

Motel. A group of people who did not want African American children to go to school with whites forced her boss to fire all of the women who had signed the lawsuit. Mrs. Briggs said the boss "asked . . . that we take our names off the petition in order to work. . . . I told him 'no,' I didn't want to do that because we would be hurting the children, and I'd rather give up my job."[7]

Thurgood Marshall had a tough decision to make before the case began. Should he argue for equal schools, or should he argue that segregated schools were against the law? He eventually decided that it was best to fight against segregation. He would argue that separate schools hurt black and white children. He would do this by using the research and expert opinions of people like Dr. Kenneth Clark and Dr. Mamie Clark.

The Clarks were psychologists who studied how racism influenced children's self-esteem. Marshall asked Dr. Kenneth Clark to test some of the children in Clarendon County, South Carolina, to see if racism had influenced how they felt about themselves. Dr. Clark's test, called the doll test, involved identical dolls, two white and two black. During the test, Dr. Clark told the

Harry and Liza Briggs had five children. Mr. Briggs had served in the U.S. Navy during World War II. The couple risked their jobs and their lives to fight for desegregation.

Harry and Liza Briggs

Dr. Clark observes as an African American boy determines which doll is better, based on the doll's appearance.

Dr. Clark attended Howard University during the 1930s. By the time he testified at the Briggs trial, he and his wife had given the doll test to about 400 children. He believed most of the African American children who took the test did not believe they were as good as white people.

sixteen students, who were between six and nine years old, to do the following: "Give me the doll you like best." "Give me the doll that is the nice doll." "Give me the doll that looks bad." "Give me the doll that is a nice color."[8] Most of the students chose the white dolls when asked to choose the doll they liked best. Dr. Clark said this suggested that the African American students believed white skin color was better than their skin color. Marshall believed the results of the doll test would be enough evidence to win the case, but it was not.

Briggs v. Elliott was argued in Charleston, South Carolina, in 1951 before three judges. Though Marshall argued passionately that segregation was unconstitutional, the judges did not agree. But they did agree that African American schools were not equal to white schools. The schools would remain segregated. The school district was told to provide equal schools for African American students. Unhappy with the court's decision, Marshall appealed the case to the United States Supreme Court. Next, the NAACP lawyers traveled to Topeka, Kansas, where they had already begun talking to families who were interested in fighting against segregated schools.

FYInfo
FOR YOUR INFORMATION

Educating African Americans Before *Brown*

During slavery, it was against the law to teach slaves to read and write, and slaves were punished when they were caught trying to learn. Yet, some slaves found ways to educate themselves and others.

In the North, free African Americans and their supporters created schools. One of the earliest schools for slaves was opened in 1704 by Elias Neau. Years later, a preacher named Richard Allen "opened a day school for children and a night school for adults . . . in Philadelphia."[9] In 1787, Prince Hall, an abolitionist, opened a school for children in his home in Boston. Later that same year, the African Free School was opened in New York. Some say the African Free School is the first free school that was not connected to a religious group.

Once African Americans in the North were freed from slavery, they were often allowed to attend public schools paid for by the government, but there were laws that said African American children were to be educated separately from white children.

When slavery ended, the number of opportunities for former slaves to become educated grew. During Reconstruction, the Freedmen's Bureau created programs that helped former slaves. One of the programs offered free education for children and adults.

Prince Hall

After Reconstruction, in 1877 the Freedmen's Bureau closed, and the South became completely segregated. African Americans and whites had separate water fountains, seating areas, public rest rooms, and schools. An African American named Homer Plessy decided to challenge segregation by sitting in the white section of a train in Louisiana. He was taken to jail and fined for breaking the law. In a court case known as *Plessy v. Ferguson*, the Supreme Court ruled that segregation was legal. Laws stated that schools must be separate and equal, but often they were not equal. In the *Brown* case, the Supreme Court had to decide if a segregated school system hurt African American children and if the *Plessy v. Ferguson* ruling that kept African Americans and whites separate was wrong.

Linda Brown and her little sister, Terry Lynn Brown, wait outside the doors of Monroe Elementary School.

Today, the Brown v. Board of Education National Historic Site is housed in the old elementary school.

Brown v. Board of Education of Topeka, Kansas

Kansas has an interesting history. Before the Civil War it was not a state; it was a territory. Abolitionists created communities such as Topeka to serve as anti-slavery areas. Once settlers began to farm in Kansas, some wanted to use slaves to help prepare the land for crops, but slavery was not allowed in Kansas Territory. Before long, people for and against slavery began fighting over control of Kansas. Soon the territory became known as "Bleeding Kansas." It did not become a state until after the Civil War began, and it still did not welcome slavery. Despite the fight to keep slavery out of Kansas, Kansas citizens created laws that supported segregation.

Kansas began segregating its schools in larger cities during the 1860s. By 1868, Kansas had accepted the Fourteenth Amendment. This amendment says that all citizens should be treated equally under the law and that all people born (or who obtain citizenship) in the United States are citizens of the country and the state in which they live, and that they should have the same rights. Even though Kansas seemed to accept the Fourteenth Amendment, it also passed laws that spread segregated schooling. Even smaller cities in Kansas such as Topeka began segregating its schools.

In 1876, laws were made that said the state's schools should desegregate. But desegregation did not last. By 1879, after large numbers of African Americans began settling in Kansas, the state decided to resegregate its elementary schools, while leaving its high schools integrated. In 1903, an African American man named William Reynolds tried to enroll his son in a white school in Topeka, Kansas, but the child was not admitted. When Reynolds sued the school board, the court explained that in two court cases, *Roberts v. the City of*

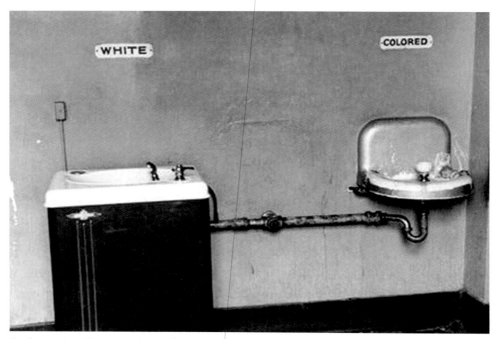

Before the *Brown* ruling of 1954, African Americans and whites were required to use separate water fountains and other public facilities.

Boston and *Plessy v. Ferguson*, the Supreme Court ruled that segregation was legal. More than forty years later, another African American man tried to enroll his child in a school for whites only. His name was Oliver Brown.

During the 1950s when Brown's daughters were attending school, Topeka, Kansas, was still segregated. It had "eighteen elementary schools for whites and four for blacks."[1] African Americans had one hotel and one movie theater, and the movie theater for whites required African Americans to sit in the balcony. Though unsuccessful, the NAACP and some citizens of Topeka tried to convince school officials to end segregation. African Americans were divided on the issue. Some African Americans felt school desegregation would help African American children, while others disagreed. Since the NAACP could not find many African American teachers to support the fight for school desegregation, it looked to parents.

Lucinda Todd, the NAACP branch secretary, tried to enroll her daughter Nancy in all-white Lowman Hill Elementary School. As expected, Nancy was

not allowed to attend. The NAACP eventually found twelve African Americans who were unhappy about the distance their children had to travel to get to school, when schools for white children were closer to their homes. For example, Lena Mae Carper's ten-year-old daughter had to walk four blocks to get to her bus stop, even though there were two schools for white students located about half as far from her home.[2] Once on the bus, the little girl could not find a seat because the bus was crowded.

Oliver Brown was a railroad worker and a part-time preacher. He had a wife and three daughters. The Browns lived in a neighborhood that was multicultural. Their neighbors were Mexican, African American, Indian, and white, but the elementary school closest to their neighborhood was for whites only. Brown's oldest daughter, Linda Carol, attended the Monroe School for African American children. Linda had to leave home at 7:40 A.M., and, according to Kluger, "walk between . . . train tracks for half a dozen blocks."[3] Her school was on the other side of the Rock Island Line switching yards, where employees worked on large trains. Linda would usually get to her bus pickup point by 8:00 A.M., but oftentimes the bus was late and she had to wait outside, even during the cold winter. When the bus arrived on time, Linda traveled for thirty minutes before finally arriving at Monroe School by 8:30 A.M. Since the school did not open until 9:00 A.M., Linda had to stand outside for thirty minutes.

Just before Linda was to begin third grade, her father received a flyer telling parents to register their children for the Sumner School, the all-white school seven blocks from the Browns' home. Though Brown knew the flyer was meant for white parents only, he tried to enroll Linda, but was refused. Angry, Brown went to the NAACP for help. The NAACP developed a lawsuit against the Board of Education in Topeka, Kansas. The lawsuit was called *Brown v. Board of Education of Topeka*, but Brown was not the only parent included in the lawsuit.

The *Brown v. Board of Education* trial began on June 25, 1951, only a few weeks after the *Briggs* trial in Charleston, South Carolina. Robert Carter, Thurgood Marshall's top assistant, and Jack Greenberg were the NAACP lawyers who argued the case.[4] Children such as Lena Mae Carper's daughter, Katherine Carper, testified in court to describe their long and uncomfortable trips to school. The NAACP lawyers argued that the schools for African Americans were not as good as the schools for white children. As in the *Briggs*

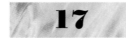

case, the lawyers also used expert opinions from psychologists and professors to tell the court that separate schools for African American children were harmful because separate schools made the children feel like they were not as good as white children. Hugh W. Speer, a professor at the University of Kansas City, told the court, "The Topeka school system . . . cannot be equal under segregation."[5] Another expert, a professor at Ohio State University named Horace B. English, agreed. He testified that if an African American person is repeatedly told "that it is unnatural for him to learn certain things [or that] he is incapable of learning, then he is less likely to learn."[6]

Brown and the others who signed the lawsuit lost the case. Judge Walter A. Huxman, the District Court judge who gave the court's opinion of the case, was not convinced that the African American schools and the white schools in Topeka, Kansas, were unequal. He said, " . . . no laws were being violated,"[7] and he dismissed the suit. Judge Huxman also pointed out that African American students used buses to get to school, while white students did not have any buses. In the end, the court used *Plessy v. Ferguson* and similar cases to decide that segregation was still legal.

However, nine "findings of fact" were attached to Judge Huxman's opinion.[8] One of the facts explained that the court agreed with psychologists who testified that segregated schools were harmful to African American children. With this fact from the court in hand, the NAACP knew it had to convince the Supreme Court to change its ruling on *Plessy v. Ferguson*. The NAACP was confident that the nine facts would help them get closer to their goal. They would keep fighting until they brought an end to segregated schools. On October 1, 1951, Brown and the NAACP lawyersappealed the case to the Supreme Court.

Lucinda and Nancy Todd

The National Association for the Advancement of Colored People (NAACP) began in January 1909 when Mary White Ovington, Dr. Henry Moskowitz, and William English Walling met in an apartment in New York to discuss how they could revive "the spirit of the abolitionists" who fought against slavery.[9] Though the Thirteenth Amendment abolished slavery in 1865, African American people were still being mistreated. Since the 100th celebration of Abraham Lincoln's birth was to take place the following month on February 12, Ovington, Moskowitz, and Walling decided to publish an article about a large meeting, or conference, they planned to hold. They would invite people from all over the country who were interested in discussing African American life and culture. Ovington, Moskowitz,

Mary White Ovington

and Walling would use the meeting to discuss how African Americans were being treated and how they could help African American people get equality.

Many people whom we celebrate today for their commitment to fighting against unfair laws supported the NAACP from the very beginning. Some of them were Jane Adams, a social worker; William Lloyd Garrison, an abolitionist; W.E.B. Du Bois, a professor; and Ida Wells Barnett, a journalist. The conference began on May 30, and it was a success. By 1910, the NAACP had hundreds of African American and white members. During their second conference in New York they elected officers, including president and secretary. Du Bois was chosen to serve as the director of publicity and research. He told the NAACP about his involvement in the Niagara Movement, a group for African Americans formed in 1905. Members of the Niagara Movement were asked to join the NAACP because both groups were doing the same type of work.

The NAACP believed it was important to use the law to fight for better conditions for African Americans. The organization began hiring lawyers as early as 1910. Many of the lawyers worked on cases about school segregation. Since the NAACP was founded, it has held fast to its commitment "to a nation-wide work for justice to the [African American] race."[10]

The Reverend L. Francis Griffin, the pas[tor]
Virginia's First Baptist Church, meets
Prince Edward County students.

*Fighting for civil rights
nearly cost the Reverend
Griffin his job as pastor, yet
he refused to stop organizing
meetings to help persuade
African Americans to support
Barbara Johns and the other
students at Moton High. Ten
years after the Brown ruling
of 1954, he sued Prince
Edward County's school
board because it tried to
avoid school desegregation.*

Davis v. County School Board of Prince Edward County

The *Davis v. County School Board of Prince Edward County* case began with teenage leaders, students at Robert R. Moton High School in Farmville, Virginia. Moton High was built in 1939 after the African American children in Prince Edward County had gone for years without a place to study after sixth grade. The school was named after Dr. Robert Russa Moton, a man from Prince Edward County who went on to become the president of Tuskegee Institute (now called Tuskegee University). The one-story Moton High was designed to hold 180 students.[1] When the school opened, 167 students enrolled. The next year, enrollment increased to 219 students. The school was not equal to white schools in the state. According to the museum dedicated to the school, it "had no gymnasium, cafeteria, lockers, or auditorium with fixed seating."[2]

With each passing year, school enrollment increased and the equipment and building became worn. By 1947, Moton High had more than twice as many students as it was designed to hold.[3] To help with the overcrowding, the county paid to have three buildings put up near Moton. The buildings provided more classrooms. Since the buildings were made out of wood and were covered with tar paper, they leaked. The buildings looked like "oversized chicken coops," and people called them "the shacks."[4]

By 1950, the number of students at Moton was 477. School officials continued to use its leaky tar paper shacks to hold some students, and they even held classes in the auditorium and on buses. The Reverend L. Francis Griffin, president of the local chapter of the NAACP, and other African American leaders tried to persuade the school board to provide a new African American school, but the school board did not provide one. When the adults

could not convince the school board, a student decided to take action. Her name was Barbara Rose Johns.

Barbara was born in New York, but her parents were from Virginia. Shortly after she was born, the family moved back to Virginia. Barbara was a quiet and shy student during her freshman and sophomore years at Moton. She was in the school chorus, student council, drama group, and clubs such as the New Homemakers of America. As she got older, she began to realize that white schools near Moton were much better than Moton High. She said, "What bothered us was the time some of the boys . . . visited . . . the white school and came back telling us how nice their whole school was. . . . The comparison made me very angry, and I remember thinking how unfair it was."[5]

During her junior year, Barbara organized a student strike. First, she went to the student leaders at the school to get their support and help with carrying out her plan. Next, she arranged for the entire student body to meet in the auditorium. Twenty-four teachers and 450 students sat in the auditorium when the stage curtains opened and revealed Barbara and the student strike committee. Barbara asked the teachers to leave. (Before the students entered the auditorium, she had already found a way to get the principal to leave the school.)

Once the adults were gone, Barbara asked the students to join her on a strike to demand a better school.[6] She said, "Look at the white school just down the road. . . . The white students have a real gymnasium, up-to-date science labs, and shiny new buses."[7] The students listened closely. Many of them shared Barbara's opinion but did not know how to convince the school board to improve Moton High. "We have to walk out now," she told them, "and not come back until white leaders have agreed to make improvements. We must strike for a better education!"[8]

The students agreed, and they stuck to the plan even when the principal returned to school and tried to talk them out of rebelling. The Reverend Griffin helped the students by giving them the name and address of NAACP lawyers in Richmond, Virginia. Barbara and the school president, Carrie Stokes, wrote to the NAACP for help. The students also went to the chairman of the county school board and the superintendent of schools, but they would not help them.

Barbara Rose Johns in 1979

When Barbara led the students to strike in 1951, she had no idea she would help change how children across the United States were educated.

Oliver Hill and Spottswood Robinson III, NAACP lawyers, got involved. They visited Farmville, Virginia, on the third day of the student strike. The lawyers had planned to talk the students out of striking, but seeing the work Barbara and the other students had accomplished made them change their minds. Hill said, "[W]e just didn't have the heart to tell 'em to break it up," to tell them to end the strike and go back to school.[9]

Barbara wanted the African American students at her school to get a good education, and she was not afraid to fight for it. Years later, someone asked her if she had been afraid when she led the strike, and she said she was not afraid. Barbara was angry. According to Anthony B. Lewis, she was "so angry, in fact, that she was willing to do something reckless, even dangerous."[10]

At first, the Moton High students were asking for equal schools. By 1951, the NAACP had decided that it would no longer accept cases that argued for equal schools in a segregated school system. All of the NAACP cases about school segregation had to fight segregation itself. The students agreed to change their argument from a call for equal schools to a request for desegregated schools. Desegregating schools would put an end to laws that excluded students from schools because of their race. Barbara said that the thought of fighting for school desegregation "seemed like reaching for the moon."[11]

After the strike, Barbara's family was afraid for her safety. They sent her to live in Montgomery, Alabama, with her uncle, Vernon Johns. Johns was a respected pastor of the Dexter Avenue Baptist Church, the same church that would hire Dr. Martin Luther King Jr. in 1954.

Spottswood Robinson filed a lawsuit in Richmond in May of 1951 on behalf of 117 high school students who "asked the state of Virginia to abolish its [order] of segregated schools."[12] A ninth grader named Dorothy E. Davis was the first plaintiff listed, so the case was called *Davis v. County School Board of Prince Edward County*. After the case was filed, Robinson traveled to Charleston, South Carolina, to attend the *Briggs* trial.

Before the *Davis* trial began, a group of white leaders tried to convince African American leaders to drop the lawsuit. The African American leaders refused. Wanting to prove in court that African American schools were equal to white schools, Prince Edward County began building a new high school for African American students.

The *Davis* case began on February 25, 1952. Robinson and the other NAACP lawyers had two arguments. First, they argued that the African American and white schools in Virginia were unequal. Next, they said segregation was unconstitutional. Even after providing the court with expert testimonies and convincing evidence, the NAACP lost the *Davis* case. The judges ruled that separate schools for blacks and whites were not in place because of racism. They said separate schools existed because citizens in the South wanted segregated schools; they were a part of southern tradition. The judges also agreed that the African American schools and the schools for whites were unequal. The judges ordered the school officials in Prince Edward County to make the African American schools equal to white schools.

Robinson appealed to the Supreme Court. The Supreme Court had already decided the year before to hear *Brown and Briggs v. Clarendon County* at the same time. Later, the Court added *Davis v. County School Board of Prince Edward County* and two other cases: *Gebhart v. Belton* and *Bolling v. Sharpe*.

On July 21, 2008, a monument honoring the leaders who worked to get Farmville, Virginia, to desegregate its schools during the 1950s was shown for the first time. The monument was dedicated on the Capitol grounds in Richmond, Virginia, and is a part of the Virginia Civil Rights Memorial. This memorial is the first monument on Capitol Square to honor women and African Americans. Made of bronze and granite, it was created by sculptor Stanley Bleifeld. When explaining the memorial he created, Bleifeld says,

> My idea was that people had to walk around this, that they couldn't get the idea from any one particular view. My idea was on one side to honor the people and to suggest the history of the original school strike. And then, on the end, there is a figure of a minister who was very helpful to the children, who gave them a lot of courage while they went on the strike. On the other end are the two lawyers who were instrumental in winning the case for *Brown v. Board of Education*. Then the other side . . . is young people . . . with books . . . all going forward, the idea being that they were going forward into an education.[13]

Barbara Johns, Oliver W. Hill Sr., Spottswood W. Robinson III, and the Reverend L. Francis Griffin are among the 18 figures in the memorial.

The monument honoring the strikers tells everyone that the state of Virginia is sorry it did not offer African American students equal schools and that it did not immediately obey the 1954 Supreme Court ruling of *Brown v. Board of Education*. A quote on the memorial from Justice Thurgood Marshall reads, "The legal system can force open doors and sometimes even knock down walls, but it cannot build bridges. That job belongs to you and me."[14] Marshall's words remind everyone that forgiveness and kindness are important tools for healing and moving forward.

Virginia Civil Rights Memorial, Farmville, Virginia

African American children learn to read at an elementary school in Washington, D.C.

Many of the all-black schools in Washington, D.C., were closed after the Brown ruling, but some buildings, including Alexander Crummell School and Military Road School, have been preserved.

Bolling v. Sharpe and Gebhart v. Belton

Bolling v. Sharpe and *Gebhart v. Belton* were added to the Supreme Court case known as *Brown v. Board of Education of Topeka, Kansas*, only a few weeks before the trial was scheduled to begin. They developed in two different places. *Bolling v. Sharpe* was argued in Washington, D.C., while *Gebhart v. Belton* began as two court cases in Delaware called *Belton v. Gebhart* and *Bulah v. Gebhart*.

African Americans in Washington, D.C., wanted equal schools for their children just as the parents did in Clarendon County, South Carolina, and Topeka, Kansas. In Washington, D.C., in 1947, Gardner Bishop formed a group called the Consolidated Parents Group, Inc. In the beginning, the group members wanted their children to be allowed to attend white schools when African American schools were too crowded. For example, Browne Junior High had to have two school sessions so that all of the African American students assigned to it could go to school while, according to Kluger, "nearby Eliot Junior High for whites had several hundred unoccupied places."[1] Browne Junior High was so crowded, Kluger continues, that school officials decided to allow some of the students to attend classes in "two rundown white schools" several blocks away.[2] The students had to walk in good and bad weather to get to their classes in the other buildings.

The Fourteenth Amendment did not apply to citizens in the District of Columbia. Only citizens of states could benefit from the Fourteenth Amendment. This did not stop Charles Hamilton Houston from acting on behalf of D.C.'s citizens. While working with Bishop's group, Houston planned to file lawsuits

Charles Hamilton Houston

Houston made a film titled **A Study of Educational Inequalities in South Carolina.** *The film captured how unequal black and white schools were in the 1930s.*

"calling for improvement at every level of learning: kindergarten classes had to be offered to black children if they were offered to white children; elementary-school class sizes had to be the same; [African American] senior-high schools were entitled to all the equipment, courses, classroom space, and athletic facilities that the white ones had."[3]

Unfortunately, Houston got sick in 1949. Even though he could not work, he was still concerned about school segregation. He told Bishop to get help from James M. Nabrit Jr., a professor of law at Howard University. When Bishop visited Nabrit to ask him to help the Consolidated Parents Group sue for equal schools, Nabrit said no. After a moment, he explained that he would take the case only if Bishop would find a group of people who were willing to sue against school segregation. Bishop agreed.

At the beginning of the school year in 1950, Bishop tried to enroll eleven African American students in the brand-new all-white John Philip Sousa Junior High. School officials refused to allow their enrollment, and the eleven

students sued. Spottswood Thomas Bolling Jr. was the first name on the suit against C. Melvin Sharpe, the president of the Board of Education of the District of Columbia. Nabrit filed *Bolling v. Sharpe* in 1951, but when the case went to trial, he did not win.

The NAACP lawyers had more success in Delaware. The first case, *Belton v. Gebhart,* is named after Ethel Belton and the members of the State Board of Education. The school board members were listed in alphabetical order, so Francis B. Gebhart's name appears first. The case developed when African American students living in Claymont, Delaware, had to travel nearly an hour by bus to Howard High School in the city of Wilmington. Yet white students in Claymont enjoyed a school close to their homes that had a variety of courses and afterschool activities. Students at Claymont could take public speaking, economics, Spanish, and advanced math, but similar courses were not offered at Howard High School.

Ethel Belton and seven other African American parents went to Louis Redding, an attorney who grew up in the area, for help. He told them to ask

John Philip Sousa
Junior High School

the State Board of Education to allow their children to attend the school in Claymont, but they were not allowed. Belton and the parents sued.

The other case, *Bulah v. Gebhart*, developed in Hockessin, Delaware. Sarah Bulah had to drive her daughter Shirley two miles to a one-room schoolhouse, while white students attended a modern school.[4] A bus for white children passed Bulah's house every day, but school officials refused to provide bus transportation for African American students. Bulah wrote to the Department of Public Instruction for Delaware. She tried to get the department to provide transportation for African American students, but they refused. She even wrote the governor of Delaware. When school officials still refused to provide buses, Bulah also went to Redding for help. Redding said he would help only if Bulah would sue for integration rather than transportation. Bulah wrote another letter. This time her letter went to the local school board, and it asked them to enroll Shirley into the all-white school near her home. Her request was denied.

Sarah Bulah and her husband, Fred, took Redding's advice and decided to sue the school board for integration. None of the African American people in Bulah's town joined their lawsuit.

When the cases went to trial, Redding and Jack Greenberg turned to Dr. Kenneth Clark again. This time Dr. Clark used the dolls to test forty-one African American children in Delaware. Clark said the test provided "clearcut evidence of rather deep damage to the self-esteem" of the students.[5]

The court agreed that separate schools in Delaware were not equal. The judge ruled that African American students should be admitted to white elementary and high schools. This was the first call for integration at the elementary and secondary level. Delaware's Attorney General, Albert Young, appealed the case. When the cases were heard in the Supreme Court, the case was called *Gebhart v. Belton*. Delaware was the last state to become a part of the Supreme Court case *Brown v. Board of Education of Topeka, Kansas*. The five cases— *Briggs v. Clarendon County*; *Brown v. Board of Education of Topeka, Kansas*; *Davis v. County School Board of Prince Edward County*; *Gebhart v. Belton*; and *Bolling v. Sharpe*—were called *Brown v. Board of Education of Topeka, Kansas*, because *Brown* was the first case the Court would address.

Howard University and its school of law were at the center of the *Brown* case. Founded by the Freedmen's Bureau in 1867, Howard University is one of the nation's most prestigious historically African American colleges and universities. In 1869, Howard University School of Law began with six students. Charles Hamilton Houston, one of the key people who helped make the *Brown* case possible, was a professor and dean of the law school. Houston mentored many of the civil rights lawyers who worked on the case, including Thurgood Marshall and Spottswood Robinson III.

Thurgood Marshall graduated as the valedictorian of Howard University School of Law in 1933. A few years later, Houston asked Marshall to work with him on a number of cases that helped lay the groundwork for the *Brown* case. Spottswood Robinson III—one of the NAACP lawyers who worked on *Davis v. County School Board of Prince Edward County*—graduated from Howard's law school in 1939. He went on to serve on Howard's faculty and work as the dean of its School of Law.

Other key figures who helped to pave the way for an affirmative *Brown* ruling were faculty members at Howard. William Hastie served on the law school faculty at Howard and worked alongside Houston and Marshall on cases that led up to the *Brown* case. James M. Nabrit Jr. was the lead lawyer who worked on the *Bolling v. Sharpe* court case, which would become a part of the *Brown* case. Later, Nabrit served as the dean of Howard University School of Law and served two terms as the university's president.

Today, Howard University is recognized for contributing to the accomplishments of professionals in many fields, including education, nursing, business, and social work, but it still boasts about the impact the university and its law school had on the *Brown* case before and after the ruling.

Main building of Howard University, 1900

The six children involved in the *Br...*
(from left to right): Vicki Hende...
Henderson, Linda Brown, James Emanu...
and Katherine Carper.

*The children were brought
together when the Supreme
Court heard the case in 1952.*

The Supreme Court Ruling

By the time the Supreme Court heard the five cases in 1952, Thurgood Marshall had already been a part of fifteen Supreme Court cases and had won thirteen of them. He and the other attorneys practiced what they would say to the Court before an audience at Howard University School of Law. The faculty, staff, and students were happy to help.

On December 9, 1952, when the actual case began, the Supreme Court was crowded, with 300 people seated and 400 people in line waiting to enter. Each side of each case had one hour to present its position. The first case was *Brown v. Board of Education of Topeka, Kansas*. Robert Carter argued for the NAACP while Paul Wilson argued for Kansas. Carter told the Court that unequal schools were unconstitutional. When it was Wilson's turn to argue, he said school segregation was allowed in the state, but it was not mandatory, and it only concerned twenty schools in Kansas. He also said that the expert testimonies about the harmful effects of segregation on African American children did not relate to the plaintiffs in Kansas because they were not tested.

Next, the Court listened to *Briggs v. Clarendon County*. Just as Carter did, Marshall argued that segregated schools were unconstitutional. Instead of asking Dr. Clark to testify about the results of his doll tests, Marshall felt it was best to give the Court a written summary of Dr. Clark's research. Other experts signed the written summary in support of Dr. Clark's opinion. A respected lawyer named John W. Davis was the lawyer for the state of South Carolina. Davis brought up the mixed opinions of school desegregation that existed in African American communities. He said respected leaders such as W.E.B. Du Bois did not believe school desegregation would help African American students.

Spottswood Robinson was the NAACP lawyer who argued in the *Davis v. County School Board of Prince Edward County* case. Robinson said since the African American schools in Prince Edward County were in poor condition, the African American students should quickly be admitted into the white schools. He also said school officials should stop using race to determine which school a child should attend. Justin Moore, the attorney for the school board, said that when the board tried to make plans to build a new school for African Americans, the students' strike interrupted those plans. He also said Virginia did not agree with findings that claimed segregation harmed African American children.

James M. Nabrit Jr. and George Edward Chalmers Hayes argued against Milton Korman, the lawyer for Washington, D.C., in the *Bolling v. Sharpe* case. Hayes went first. He said Congress did not make school segregation mandatory in Washington, D.C., and that the officials in Washington chose to have segregated schools. Nabrit said American citizens had rights that must be protected. According to Nabrit, if Congress or states tried to take those rights, the Supreme Court was supposed to step in and correct them. Korman argued that Washington, D.C., had the right to have segregated schools. He went on to argue that after the Civil War, Congress believed it had to help ex-slaves by giving them schools, but it did not believe integrated schools were right for African American students. Korman also said Congress believed African American students would feel uncomfortable in schools with whites who did not want them there.

Attorney General Albert Young argued first when it was time to talk about *Gebhart v. Belton*. He said Delaware had planned to make Howard High, the African American school, and Claymont High, the white school, equal. Similar to the other lawyers who argued against integration, Young said that the harmful effects of segregation on African American children did not relate to the plaintiffs in Delaware. The NAACP lawyers, Louis Redding and Jack Greenberg, said the judge in Delaware was right to order school desegregation. They also said desegregation, which had started at the beginning of the school year, was working well.

On the morning of December 13, 1952, the judges had not reached a decision, so they met to discuss the cases. Some researchers say that it seemed as if Chief Justice Fred M. Vinson and a few of the other justices were going

to rule that segregation was legal, or constitutional. At the beginning of 1953, some of the judges still believed that schools should remain segregated, while others felt segregated schools were unfair. The judges asked the lawyers to re-argue their cases in the fall of 1953. They wanted the lawyers to talk more about their cases and how the Fourteenth Amendment related to the desegregation of schools.

When Chief Justice Vinson died in September of 1953, President Dwight D. Eisenhower asked Earl Warren, the former governor of California, to take Vinson's place, and the trial continued. Finally, the *Brown v. Board of Education of Topeka, Kansas*, opinion was read on Monday, May 17, 1954. The Court ruled that segregated schools were against the law; schools must desegregate. No student could be denied admission to a school based on his or her race.

In the *Brown* ruling, the Supreme Court said, "We conclude that in the field of public education the doctrine of 'separate but equal' has no place. Separate educational facilities are . . . unequal."[1] After the opinion was read,

W.E.B. Du Bois

W.E.B. Du Bois wrote a number of books and articles that argued that all Americans deserve equal rights.

Louis Redding (left) consults with Thurgood Marshall during the *Gebhart v. Belton* case. Redding was the first African American lawyer to practice law in Delaware. He was instrumental in desegregating the University of Delaware in 1950.

Justice Warren said the court would listen to arguments about how the schools would desegregate.

In 1954, right after the Brown ruling, seventeen states—Alabama, Arkansas, Delaware, Florida, Georgia, Kentucky, Louisiana, Maryland, Mississippi, Missouri, North Carolina, Oklahoma, South Carolina, Tennessee, Texas, Virginia, and West Virginia—and Washington, D.C., had laws that supported segregation. Thurgood Marshall suggested that desegregation begin immediately, but in *Brown II*, the decision that explained how and when school desegregation would take place (ruled on May 31, 1955), the Court decided

that school divisions in the South should develop desegregation plans and carry them out "with all deliberate speed."[2] Some school districts, including those in Washington, D.C., Baltimore, St. Louis, and West Virginia, developed integration plans shortly after the *Brown* decision was read, while others fought against school desegregation.

When African Americans tried to enroll in previously all-white schools, they were met with resistance. The entire world watched as nine students in Little Rock, Arkansas, tried to integrate Central High School in 1957, only to face an angry mob. Eventually, during the 1958–1959 school year, the governor of Arkansas closed the schools. School districts like the one in Prince Edward County, Virginia, where Barbara Johns had led a student strike, followed the governor of Arkansas's lead. J. Lindsay Almond Jr., the governor of Virginia, closed other schools in Virginia too, including schools in Richmond, Charlottesville, and Norfolk. The schools in Prince Edward County were closed from 1959 to 1964 to avoid school desegregation.

Integrating schools was not easy even after *Brown*. The *Brown II* ruling ensured integration plans would be implemented quickly.

Oliver Brown, father of Linda and Terry Lynn Brown, for whom the *Brown* case was named

Mrs. Nettie Hunt and her daughter, Nikie, sit on the steps of the Supreme Court building following the *Brown* verdict.

Elizabeth Eckford (left) was so hurt by her experience at Central High she was unable to speak publicly about it until the 1990s. Hazel Bryan Massery, one of the women behind Eckford, eventually apologized to Elizabeth for trying to keep her from attending all-white Central.

Linda Brown Smith, Harry Briggs Jr., Spottswood Bolling Jr., and Ethel Louise Belton Brown celebrate the 10th anniversary of the *Brown* trial in 1964 at the Hotel Americana.

The Civil Rights Act of 1964, which says segregation is illegal, encouraged school districts to desegregate. Part of the act allowed the Department of Health, Education, and Welfare to find out whether schools had desegregated. The act also allowed the government to deny federal funding to local school districts that did not meet federal guidelines for integration. After the act was put in place, schools in southern states began integrating.

The fight for school desegregation has been, and continues to be, a long and hard one. Segregation in U.S. schools still exists in Colorado, Connecticut, Rhode Island, and Massachusetts. Some people debate the influence *Brown* has had on improving education for all students, but *Brown* influenced much more than education. It helped rid the United States of segregation in all areas of public life. Separate rest rooms, water fountains, or movie theaters do not exist today largely because of Brown. This important case changed education in the United States and sparked movement toward equality for all Americans.

Chief Justice Earl Warren

FYInfo
FOR YOUR INFORMATION

The Little Rock Nine with Daisy Bates, their mentor and president of the Arkansas NAACP

Integrating Central High School

In 1957, Little Rock, Arkansas, had four high schools. One school, Horace Mann, was for African Americans. The other schools—Hall, a technical high school, and Central—were for whites. After the *Brown* ruling, school officials in Little Rock made plans to desegregate. Little Rock's superintendent of schools, Virgil Blossom, and other school officials chose the African American students they wanted to interview from a list of teenagers interested in being among the first to attend the previously all-white schools. The superintendent dissuaded some students from attending Central, while other students decided on their own not to pursue integration. When the process was over, ten students were chosen to integrate Central: Jane Hill, Minnijean Brown, Elizabeth Eckford, Ernest Green, Thelma Mothershed, Melba Pattillo, Gloria Ray, Terrence Roberts, Jefferson Thomas, and Carlotta Walls. Jane Hill eventually decided to return to an all–African American high school, reducing the number of students to nine.

On September 4, when the students walked toward the school building, a row of National Guardsmen blocked the entrance. It took several weeks and persuasion from President Dwight D. Eisenhower to get Arkansas Governor Orval Faubus to allow the African American students into Central.

Once the students were allowed in, white students bothered them throughout the school day. The Little Rock Nine were poked with safety pins, sprayed with ink, thrown into lockers, shoved, and tripped. The students had been taught how to use nonviolent resistance. If someone tripped them or called them names, they were to remain calm and respectful. Sometimes the harassment was too difficult for the nine to ignore. After repeatedly being called names and shoved, Minniejean Brown defended herself and was suspended.

When the school year ended, Ernest Green became the first African American student to graduate from Central High. In 1999, over forty years after the Little Rock Nine integrated Central High School, the nine African Americans received the highest civilian award in the country, the Congressional Gold Medal.

Chronology

1850 In *Roberts v. City of Boston*, Chief Justice Lemuel Shaw says segregated schools are legal.

1865 The Thirteenth Amendment says slavery is illegal.

1867 Howard University begins.

1868 The Fourteenth Amendment secures citizenship rights for every American, including African Americans.

1887 Florida and other states in the South pass laws that require segregation.

1879 Kansas decides to resegregate its elementary schools.

1896 The Supreme Court decides *Plessy v. Ferguson*. The Court says separate-but-equal facilities for African Americans and whites are legal.

1903 William Reynolds tries to enroll his son in a white school in Topeka, Kansas, but is denied because he is African American.

1909 The National Association for the Advancement of Colored People (NAACP) is established.

1933 Thurgood Marshall graduates from Howard University's School of Law. He is first in his class. Oliver Hill is second.

1936 Thurgood Marshall joins the NAACP's legal team.

1940 The (NAACP) Legal Defense and Educational Fund is founded.

1950 Charles Hamilton Houston dies.

1951 Barbara Rose Johns leads a student strike at Robert R. Moton High School in Prince Edward County, Virginia.

1952 The Supreme Court hears the five cases that make up *Brown v. Board of Education of Topeka, Kansas*.

1954 In *Brown v. Board of Education of Topeka, Kansas*, the Supreme Court says schools in the United States should be desegregated.

1955 In *Brown II*, ruled on May 31, the Court says school districts should develop desegregation plans and carry them out "with all deliberate speed."

1957 Nine students integrate Central High School in Little Rock, Arkansas.

1958 Central High School graduates its first African American student: Ernest Green.

1959 Prince Edward County, Virginia, closes its schools to avoid desegregation.

1964 President Lyndon B. Johnson signs the Civil Rights Act of 1964.

1971 The Supreme Court ruling in *Swann v. Charlotte-Mecklenburg Board of Education* says school districts should use busing to help integrate the schools.

1986 The Supreme Court says the school districts that have integrated no longer have to use desegregation plans.

1991 Barbara Rose Johns dies.

1995 The Supreme Court says school districts can have local control of schools.

2002 The Civil Rights Project at Harvard University finds that schools are resegregating.

2004 The 50th anniversary of *Brown v. Board of Education of Topeka, Kansas*, is celebrated.

2007 The 50th anniversary of school integration at Central High School in Little Rock, Arkansas, is celebrated.

2008 A memorial honoring Virginia civil rights activists, including Barbara Rose Johns, is dedicated.

2009 New Haven, Connecticut, firefighters take a test for promotions. The test is declared racially biased against African Americans, and the test is thrown out. White Americans who passed the test claim reverse discrimination and take their case to the Supreme Court.

Timeline in History

1854 Ashmun Institution, the first African American college, opens.

1861 The Civil War begins.

1863 President Abraham Lincoln reads the Emancipation Proclamation.

1865 The Civil War ends and the Freedmen's Bureau is founded.

1866 Ashmun Institution is renamed Lincoln University in honor of President Abraham Lincoln.

1869 Howard University Law School opens with six students.

1872 Howard University graduates the first African American woman lawyer, Charlotte E. Ray.

1876 Reconstruction ends.

1929 Civil rights leader Martin Luther King Jr. is born.

1955 Montgomery Bus Boycott begins in Alabama.

1956 Autherine Lucy is admitted to the University of Alabama.

1961 The Freedom Riders travel south to help end discrimination on buses.

1962 James Meredith, the first African American student to enroll in the University of Mississippi, is escorted to class by United States Marshals.

1967 Thurgood Marshall becomes the first African American Supreme Court Justice.

1973 Vietnam War ends.

1976 Black History Week is extended to Black History Month.

1990 Douglas Wilder becomes the governor of Virginia. He is the first African American to be elected governor in the United States.

1991 Clarence Thomas becomes the second African American Supreme Court Justice.

2006 Ceremonial groundbreaking takes place on the National Mall in Washington, D.C., for the Dr. Martin Luther King, Jr. Memorial.

2009 Barack Obama becomes the first African American U.S. president.

Chapter Notes

Chapter One: *Briggs v. Clarendon County, South Carolina*

1. Walter G. Stephan, "A Brief Historical Overview of School Desegregation," in *School Desegregation: Past, Present, and Future*, ed. Walter G. Stephan and Joe R. Feagin (New York: Plenum Press, 1980), p. 11.
2. Richard Kluger, *Simple Justice: The History of Brown v. Board of Education and Black America's Struggle for Equality* (New York, Vintage, 2004), p. 7.
3. Ibid., p. 14.
4. Ibid.
5. Ibid.
6. Ibid., p. 18.
7. Juan Williams, *Eyes on the Prize: America's Civil Rights Years, 1954–1965* (New York: Viking, 1987), p. 19.
8. Kluger, p. 317.
9. Lerone Bennett, Jr., *Before the Mayflower: A History of Black America*, 7th ed. (Chicago: Johnson, 1982), p. 83.

Chapter Two: *Brown v. Board of Education of Topeka, Kansas*

1. Richard Kluger, *Simple Justice: The History of Brown v. Board of Education and Black America's Struggle for Equality* (New York: Vintage, 2004), p. 375.
2. Ibid., p. 407.
3. Ibid., p. 409.
4. Juan Williams, *Eyes on the Prize: America's Civil Rights Years, 1954-1965* (New York: Viking, 1987), p. 24.
5. Ibid.
6. Ibid.
7. Ibid.
8. Kluger, p. 425.
9. Mary White Ovington, "How the NAACP Began," http://www.naacp.org/about/history/howbegan/index.htm
10. Ibid.

Chapter 3: *Davis v. County School Board of Prince Edward County*

1. Richard Kluger, *Simple Justice: The History of Brown v. Board of Education and Black America's Struggle for Equality* (New York: Vintage, 2004), p. 460.
2. Robert Russa Moton Museum, "Historical Background," http://www.motonmuseum.org/history.htm.
3. Kluger, p. 460.
4. Ibid., p. 461.
5. Ibid., p. 467.
6. Andrew B. Lewis, "A Brief History of Prince Edward County's School Desegregation Fight," http://www.vacivilrightsmemorial.org/facts/documents/CRMFMotonABrief History-8pageversion.doc
7. Ibid.
8. Ibid.
9. Kluger, p. 477.
10. Lewis.
11. Kluger, p. 477.
12. Juan Williams, *Eyes on the Prize: America's Civil Rights Years, 1954–1965* (New York: Viking, 1987), p. 27.
13. Jann Malone, "A Key Moment in the Struggle—Statues Honor Pivotal Role That 1951 Student Walkout in Va. Played," *Richmond Times-Dispatch*, July 20, 2008. Retrieved from NewsBank On-line Database.

14. "Courage Enshrined," *The Free Lance-Star*, July 27, 2008. Retrieved from NewsBank On-line Database.

Chapter 4: *Bolling v. Sharpe* and *Gebhart v. Belton*
1. Richard Kluger, *Simple Justice: The History of Brown v. Board of Education and Black America's Struggle for Equality* (New York: Vintage, 2004), p. 515.
2. Ibid.
3. Ibid., p. 518.
4. Ibid., p. 435.
5. Ibid., p. 441.

Chapter 5: The Supreme Court Ruling
1. *Brown v. Board of Education*, 347 U.S. 483 (1954).
2. Lino A. Graglia, "From Prohibiting Segregation to Requiring Integration: Developments in the Law of Race and the Schools Since Brown," in *School Desegregation: Past, Present, and Future*, ed. Walter G. Stephan and Joe R. Feagin (New York: Plenum Press, 1980), p. 72.

Further Reading

For Young Adults

Good, Diane L. *Brown v. Board of Education*. New York: Children's Press, 2004.

Sharp, Anne Wallace. *Separate but Equal: The Desegregation of America's Schools*. Lucent Library on Black History. Detroit: Lucent Books, 2007.

Thomas, Joyce Carol, ed. *Linda Brown, You Are Not Alone: The Brown v. Board of Education Decision*. New York: Hyperion, 2003.

Works Consulted

"About the School of Law." http://www.law.howard.edu/19

Altman, Susan. *The Encyclopedia of African-American Heritage*. New York: Facts on File, Inc., 1997.

Bennett, Lerone, Jr. *Before the Mayflower: A History of Black America*, 7th ed. Chicago: Johnson, 1982.

"Courage Enshrined." *The Free Lance-Star*. July 27, 2008. Retrieved from NewsBank On-line Database.

Gilbert, Peter. *With All Deliberate Speed: A Look at the Landmark Brown vs. the Board of Education*. DVD. Silver Spring, MD: Discovery Communications, 2004.

Hampton, Henry, and Judith Vecchione. *Eyes on the Prize: Fighting Back, 1957–1962*. DVD. Alexandria, VA: PBS, 2006.

Jones, Inez Davenport. "Students Went on Strike to Challenge Jim Crow." *The Virginian-Pilot*. August 20, 2007. Retrieved from NewsBank On-line Database.

Kendrick, Paul, and Stephen Kendrick. *Sarah's Long Walk: The Free Blacks of Boston and How Their Struggle for Equality Changed America*. Boston, Massachusetts: Beacon, 2004.

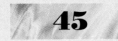

Kluger, Richard. *Simple Justice: The History of Brown v. Board of Education and Black America's Struggle for Equality*. New York: Vintage, 2004.

Lewis, Andrew B. "A Brief History of Prince Edward County's School Desegregation Fight." http://www.vacivilrightsmemorial.org/facts/documents/CMFMotonABrief History-8pageversion.doc

Lynch, Janice, and Shepard Ranbom. "Timeline: The Long, Hard Road to Educational Equality." *Educational Record*, Fall 1987–Winter 1988.

Malone, Jann. "A Key Moment in the Struggle—Statues Honor Pivotal Role That 1951 Student Walkout in Va. Played." *Richmond Times-Dispatch*. July 20, 2008. Retrieved from NewsBank On-line Database.

NAACP Legal Defense and Educational Fund. "The Winding Road to *Brown* and Beyond; An LDF Chronology of the Struggle for Educational Equity: The Legacy of *Brown v. Board of Education*. http://www.naacpldf.org/content/pdf/pubs/The_Winding_Road_to_Brown.pdf

Ovington, Mary White. "How the NAACP Began." http://www.naacp.org/about/history/howbegan/index.htm

"Robert Russa Moton Museum: Historical Background." http://www.motonmuseum.org

Stephan, Walter G., and Joe R. Feagin, ed. *School Desegregation: Past, Present, and Future*. New York: Plenum Press, 1980.

Walker, Julian. "Memorial Pays Tribute to Those Who Fought School Segregation." *The Virginian-Pilot*, July 22, 2008.

Williams, Juan. *Eyes on the Prize: America's Civil Rights Years, 1954–1965*. New York: Viking, 1987.

On the Internet

The ABCs of School Integration http://www.tolerance.org/teach/activities/activity.sp?ar=842&pa=2

Brown @ 50 http://www.brownat50.org

Civil Rights 101: School Desegregation and Equal Opportunity http://www.civilrights.org/resources/civilrights101/desegregation.html

NAACP LDF: School Integration http://www.naacpldf.org/

Robert Russa Moton Museum: Historical Background http://www.motonmuseum.org

Glossary

abolish (uh-BAH-lish)

To end something that has existed for a long time.

abolitionist (aa-buh-LIH-shuh-nist)

Someone who wants to end a law.

appealed (uh-PEELd)

Asking the court to change a decision.

defendant (dih-FEN-dent)

The person in court who is accused of breaking the law.

deliberate (di-LIH-ber-ayt)

To think about something slowly and carefully before acting.

equality (ee-KWAH-lih-tee)

Having the same rights as everyone else.

plaintiff (PLAYN-tif)

The person in court who sues someone else for breaking the law.

resistance (ree-ZIS-tants)

Refusal to accept an idea or situation as it is.

segregation (seh-greh-GAY-shun)

Separating people because of their race.

self-esteem (self-uh-STEEM)

The feeling that you are someone who deserves to be liked and respected.

sue

To take someone to court because they did something wrong.

testify (TES-tuh-fy)

To tell the truth in court.

unconstitutional (un-kon-stih-TOO-shuh-nul)

Illegal; not allowed by the U.S. Constitution.

PHOTO CREDITS: Cover, pp. 1, 3, 8, 11, 12, 16, 26, 28, 35, 36, 37, 38 (bottom), 39 (background), 41—Library of Congress; pp. 6, 14, 32—Carl Iwasaki/Getty Images; p. 20—Friends Journal; p. 23—*The Richmond Times*; p. 38 (top)—The Brown Foundation. Every effort has been made to locate all copyright holders of material used in this book. If any errors or omissions have occurred, corrections will be made in future editions of this book.

Index